Renault 30

Also available from HINCHAS PRESS:

Bringer of Culture – Jim Heavily
Buy One, Give One: Inspiring Library Stories – Oleg Kagan
Librarians with Spines – Max Macias and Yago S. Cura, eds.
Librarians with Spines Vol. II – Max Macias and Yago S. Cura, eds.
Odas a Futbolistas – Yago S. Cura & Abel M. Folgar
Tlacuilx: Tongues in Quarantine, poetry by Project 1521
X LA Poets – Linda Ravenswood, ed.

Renault 30

poems by

Abel M. Folgar

An Hinchas Press Book
Published by Hinchas de Poesía
Los Angeles

Cover Art by Daniel S. Folgar.

Printed in the United States
By IngramSpark, Lightning Source LLC
1246 Heil Quaker Blvd, La Vergne, TN 37086

Names: Folgar, Abel, 1977 - author
Title: Renault 30 / Abel Folgar
Description: Los Angeles, CA : Hinchas de Poesia Press (HINCHAS Press), [2022]
Identifiers: LOC# 2022940927 | ISBN# 978-1-954640-99-3
Subjects: Venezuela--Poetry

HINCHAS Press (Hinchas de Poesía Press) is a Los Angeles-based micropress that publishes zines, poetry, poetry in translation, and library science non-fiction. In line with the rabid fanaticism that defines *fútbol* (soccer) fans in Latin America, HINCHAS channels the best aspects of that energy and gives a voice to non-traditional and marginalized communities, supports social justice initiatives, and advocates for bilingual literacy endeavors, especially along portions of the *Américas* that are monolingual.

Learn more about HINCHAS Press (hinchaspress.com), our defunct online literary journal, *Hinchas de Poesía* (hinchasdepoesia.com), and the eternal debt of gratitude we owe to James Wright Foley (1973 – 2014), an American combat journalist that had the moral courage to report on the atrocities being committed against the Syrian people by the Assad regime.

Please direct all inquiries to:

Yago Cura, HINCHAS Press
1803 Gramercy Avenue
Torrance, CA 90501
yagoscura@gmail.com

Acknowledgements

Thanks to my family, my wife, my children – with them, everything is possible.

Special gratitude to the junior exec who took Renault to Venezuela and to my father for putting behind the memory of that LTD I ruined and buying the best damn car in the world.

To Campbell McGrath for introducing m loncar's *66 Galaxie* many moons ago and to loncar for disappearing in his own magical way immediately after publication it seems; leaving me with questions that mind, and time have turned into fantastical assumptions. I hope you're drawing word maps somewhere or having that meal at B Street Souflaki.

Well, not true... really.

Recent investigations (in 2022) place him within the halls of faculty at National Pingtung University in Taiwan, lecturing and researching writing, literature and drama.

To Yago, my homie who for decades, has kept the car gassed, the engine idling and the notion that poesy is the right lane to be in. *Hasta el fin sin frenos mi pana, dos crotos culos rotos.*

Thanks to Westly Reason for their assistance editing. To Pilar, Campbell and Yaddy for their kind words. To my brother Dan for laying this sucker out instead of sleeping.

And to Butler Waugh and Gray Kane, friends and mentors gone too soon.

Poems

My dad had a '74 Maverick that would never be as cool as a Renault 30 around the *muro* where all the *panas* of my street would gather around. But it was new, and it would be my dad's pride and joy — his triumph in a life of loss. Those were the 70s of the oil boom, where we grew up with some pride: Bolívar and oil was all we needed. But on his television show, *Valores Humanos*, acclaimed Venezuelan intellectual Arturo Uslar Pietri did tell us, his *"amigos invisibles,"* that there would be a price to pay. Nobody heard him. We actually ended up killing both. Or somebody did.

What was cool at the time was how good the cars were, how cheap the gasoline was, the roads and freeways that Pérez Jiménez built before democracy even started — and before it died. And we had Miss Universe, how could we not be a great country?

In this series of poems, these memories of the writer's youth, we are transported to a country that had untold riches, where possibilities seemed as infinite as the power of your car of choice, with cheap gas available forever and a dollar at 4,30 Bs. The promise of our land, where everything was abundant, seemed to guarantee our future, and our children's future. It wasn't to be.

Reading Abel's intimate memories of family and history brought me to a melancholic state, and I remembered that immigrants like my parents, refugees like them, prospered or at least survived well enough. They made me wish we could take the road back — in any kind of car — and do things differently, and that (the original) María Lionza, fiercely proud, would be waiting for us in the middle of the freeway with her arms stretched up towards the sun.

La Venezuela que amamos y que aún existe en otra dimensión. Gracias por el viaje.

Pilar Marrero
Journalist and author, *El despertar del sueño americano*
Los Angeles, 2022

Renault 30

ONE MORNING IN LA GUAIRA: WILLIAM HENRY PHELPS

a crazy gringo by most accounts,
broad-shouldered and dressed like a man
of business who meant business by the looks
of his knuckles, lands the biggest boat the sleepy
coastal town has ever seen and immediately,
the deep green of his gringo eyes fill
with all of the pleasures that he will take
from the sons and daughters of this land—
Europe's not gonna buy shit anytime soon
and these people are ready to move from outdated
Panhard Levassors and Cadillac B's; ready
to park their plump behinds into American
leather and cruise their tree-lined boulevards.
Drink their coffee, drink the rum, drink whatever watery
swill passes for beer around these parts.
This—the first of many boats—each one bigger
and more corpulent than the last, will flood
the country's growing veins. Yeah, he's gonna
take it all, and even if he falls in love with these
people, their *arepas*, their full-figured daughters;
he'll leave for the next mark when the bank
accounts run dry—he'll pull out every damn iron
railroad track if he has to, drown every damn
horse too if it comes to it; Ford rhymes with lord
and on this land, a lord he'll surely be.

Y ahora damas, caballeros, chamas, chamos, musiús, malandros, gafos, corruptos, invitados del 'jai sosayeti' y todo lo demás que suele caer entre las rejillas del alma – ¡a jugar pelota!

RENAULT 30

This is a machine, and it eats paint chips—
so many that they've become clogged
into an eye-clawing Jackson Pollock irritation;
slowing everything down from the accumulated
chemicals sandbagging the critical avenues
of its electrical brain. We are going to a game.
We can see it through a window but
the window somehow blocks most of the light.
We're in my dad's sandy champagne-colored
Renault 30, the greatest car ever imagined,
the greatest car ever made, the greatest
vessel for living that the gods of all religions—
in rare accordance—could ever create.
This might be the mechanized distillation of
liberté, *égalité* and *fraternité* but to us *criollos*,
in the land Bolívar made and *el muérgano de*
Chávez eventually destroys, this is the
Renól treinta in *criollo* parlance *y es tremenda*
máquina mi pana, sape gato y burda de arrecha.
We can feel everything crack under the weight
of dried organic matter. Everything's opaque.
Like a Bunsen burner jetted its flame at it.
Memory assaults the whiteness of its empty
corridors—alarming shadows in its wake.
There's a prosthetic limb caught in the
terrible moisture of a tornado somewhere.

CÚA: MARIAN DEVOTIONAL

A large blue butterfly chases a miracle
across the ruins of a farm south of Caracas.
All the Latin Virgins form from light
and appear brown-skinned, radiant, and plump
while their European versions—
having more centuries of tormenting the faithful
with lysergic delusions under their robes—
materialize from fog and look sickly,
the raw flesh of whelks, drained,
and so sinewy you can trace their veins with a pencil.
There's no almshouse at this Bethany
but it mists from the hills, the sun jumps around in fits
Ritalin couldn't control, the Host bleeds,
and an invisible choir plays a calvocanonical
game of call and response with the sweet scent
of roses no one can seem to find;
soothing like the distant dings of waterfall upon rock.
People travel here—no shells denoting their pilgrimage,
no circular requirements needed to signal completion:
por cola, by taxi, *porpuesto*, or foot,
sometimes a mix of those and for different reasons.
All personal and more deserving than the next;
may someone bring them the dream,
a petal, their breast, their hands, the earth.

MAMPOTE

We stir our *guayoyos* slowly,
the black coffee growing darker with each twirl.

Through the window,
arid hills sit unremarkable against

the morning's blue.
The dark bark of a few

araguaneys in the distance breaking
the monochromatic monotony.

Their yellow canopies,
impossible and brighter than the sun,

a rising habitat of doubted hope.
Between us, somewhere in the dip

that creases this landscape,
the highway is a sticky goop.

It's an agony without crisis,
decline and wear; maybe it will

collapse into memory, ruin, vestiges.
If its disengagement prevails, will a resurgence come?

Would anything other than this
humble cup of coffee pass without incident?

TRECE

Go ahead he says,
when we level
and straighten out,

drop it into third
and put your hand on the wheel.

He doesn't blink when
I tug a wee bit harder than
I should, bringing
the French jet a little too close
to the guardrail,
a little too close to the
precipice overlooking
the old highway—

the broken one
with faded asphalt
frozen mid-boil.

We are a reference of time,
an irreparable certainty
flirting with destruction.

You can let go now, he says,
if your mother saw this,
we'd be devoured
by a liturgy of mourning.

The Renault's electricity
keeps zapping me long after
I let go of the wheel.

The dust behind us an
unknown passage to enigmas.

GUARENAS

The freshly mowed weekend lawns
of Kendall could never replace
the thick tar of exhaust that covers
my memories of Caracas
but they did momentarily take me back,
to those Saturday mornings
we'd drive east to Guarenas,
winding down the snaky *Carretera de Petare*,
all trust placed on the Renault 30's V6
as it purred with the grace of angels.
We'd inhale breakfast in Mampote,
a *guayoyo*, tomato and scrambled eggs,
before my dad's softball games
for the Banco Unión team.
The baseball fields, vibrant from the
sward's manicure, crunchy in my throat—
clammy like an attic in my nose.
The wilderness surrounding them
a respite from the city
and clean oxygen communion—
my lungs struggling to keep up with the *libélulas*
across the outfields.
Afterwards, I'd ask if he hit *jonrones*,
making small talk during the drive back
that always felt faster and shorter;
the switchbacks rocking us gently.

Whether we left from Las Mercedes or Parque del Este,
the *ranchos* and condos were all the same—different
worlds I couldn't explore—and María Lionza on her tapir
would always bid us farewell as we glided out of Caracas
on the Autopista Francisco Fajardo towards Highway 16.
I was too young then to understand the offerings left
at the statue—even less the reasons why young and old
would brave that wide river of asphalt to pray at her feet.
The 30's V6 purr competing for attention as the tape deck
came alive with Loretta Goggi, ABBA, Hombres G, Wilfrido
Vargas or Franco De Vita from whatever Memorex was around;
and I'd drift away as Caracas became Guarenas, Guarenas
became Guatire, Guatire became Panaquire, Panaquire
became El Guapo, Clarínes, Puerto Píritu and so on until,
the outskirts of Barcelona, south of Puerto La Cruz, where he'd
point this magnificent beast south on the 16; through San Mateo,
Anaco, Cantaura, El Tigre and La Viuda—whose shared spatiality
he'd come to know so well during his college years, to
Soledad and the suspended miracle of Puente Angostura
across the Orinoco and into Ciudad Bolívar and grandpa's
guava treats and nonna's sweet, wrinkled kisses—
offerings I loved, understood, and have missed ever since.

TO BE FAIR

in case the word gets out–
    dad also drove a '72 bug

    and it was so much better
    than the '70 his uncle got him–

the bad apple that left him stranded
a handful of times on that arid stretch
between El Tigre and La Viuda on

    Highway 16,

populated by disillusioned
Marxist-Leninist *guerrilleros* from the
FALN days and always,
        always,

the day before exams at the
Universidad de Oriente in Ciudad Bolívar.

Once his uncle caved and swapped the bugs,
my old man really came to love
    and adore

    a car like it was his child—

    canary yellow exterior,
    burgundy leather inside

you'd think it was a Caddie the way he doted on it;
kept it for *el día de parada* when he couldn't
    cruise the 30 to work;

He even shed a tear decades later

    when the commie rebirth ran us out
    and he was forced to sell it to a friend—

handing over the keys and a box of
    spare red/white, American style
        taillights

a hoodlum he once sewed up

    gifted him.

Ford Motor Co. de Venezuela publishes the magazine *Aravanei* during the 1940's. The poet Juan Bautista de Jesús Liscano Velutini (1915 – 2001), founder of the literary group Summa, armed with a quick wit and a polemic disdain for bad governance, is hired as its editor.

HUGO CHÁVEZ JOINS TWITTER ON APRIL 2010

How's it going? I'm here just like I said: at midnight. I'm off to Brazil. And very happy to work for Venezuela. We will be victorious!

Que rico amanecer in Miraflores. Ready to fight for you! We will fight and triumph!

There is no problem here! Venezuela looks to the future with Bolivarian defiance! *La revolución sigue triunfando!*

Comrades! *Areperos!* We must all do our part for the revolution. Together we will conquer over imperialism!

Los yanquis didn't catch Osama. They disrespected the sovereignty of Pakistan but we'll never hear a *con permiso.*

I like baseball. A lot. #Magallanes

Chávez es un Pueblo! Chávez are millions... millions! You too are Chávez!

If you only knew about the incredible fish soup I had for lunch here in Cuba. *Y plátano maduro con arroz!* Sorry if you haven't eaten yet!

Comrades! How happy you make me! Keep fighting hard to defeat the bourgeoisie! It's pouring here in La Habana.

Does the opposition trouble me? *Eso es un safarancho.* Greatness is frequently opposed!

In La Orchila I discovered poetry, ah! What a great place to read and write. Pink sand like a flamingo's feather.

With our friends in La Habana and Teheran, we will build the most formidable machine the world has ever seen!

Los yanquis will say anything, *yo soy tremenda candanga*, next they'll claim the cancer will eat me. Nothing eats me. I eat everything.

I've seen the fruits of revolution. We will have something like it here, equal but better, we'll make Venezuela great again!

@PutinRF *oye! Cuando llegan los* AK-47's?

As a soldier I'm filled with pride by our country and our soldiers. The soldiers of Bolívar we are; the country of Bolívar we are!

A puro jonrón se comieron a los Tiburones de La Guaira! #Magallanes

Of course, I love debating. *Los Patriotas* make the opposition look ridiculous at every turn. *La revolución sigue triunfando!*

Comrades! *Areperos! Los yanquis* poisoned our cattle and livestock!

Cancer does not figure into the fight for the nation, in this way I'm a little bit capitalist.

This is an example of efficiency and *mística obrera*; in our cinder block factory building a future. Bolivarian progress.

Los yanquis are in the employ of Zionist gold. It is your duty to disregard the lies of the empire. Together we will triumph!

Comrades! *Areperos!* Lining up for milk is a revolutionary necessity in the struggle against the evil bovinity of the *yanqui* state!

Nadie puede contra los Navegantes. I love baseball so much! #Magallanes

I'm accepting your blessings. Of course I'm healthy. We will live and we will triumph. *Somos un Pueblo.*

We've arrived in Venezuela again, thank God. Thank you, my beloved *Pueblo.* We'll continue the Cuban treatments here.

Thank you, Fidel, Raúl, and all of Cuba! Thank you, Venezuela, for so much love!

Tremendo regalito que les voy a dejar! #Wholovesyoubaby

I'm soldered into Christ and confident of my doctors and nurses. To victory always! We will live and triumph!

The infinite capabilities of the Batmobile by Messrs. West, Keaton, Bale, et al. The concrete cocaine fantasy of Marty and Doc's stainless-steel DMC DeLorean zipping through Oedipal time (note: in 2005, at least ten were parked behind an office building in the vicinity of Bonita Springs, FL—ready for their next adventure). The slick innuendo of Q's tricked-out Aston Martin DB5 and the eternal disappointment of handing the keys over to the Bond du jour. The Coors-sponsored outlaw slapstick of Smokey & the Bandit's '77 Trans AM 28-hour run. The General Lee's CBS-sanctioned casual racism as them Duke boys (no relation to David, failed politico and former Grand Wizard) ran afoul of Sheriff Rosco and his cronies. The unspoken importance of Thelma & Louise's '66 Thunderbird as it flew them to fancy, out of the heat and eventually into the precipitous possibilities of their next lives. And all of the sentient ones: Chevron's cheeky British plasticine gas-guzzlers, that intrepid love bug Herbie, the jealous rage of Detroit-built Christine, KITT's calm demeanor in the face of danger, "Lightning" McQueen and all of his pals—heck, even the Magic School Bus too! But these two...

...THESE TWO GET A FREE PASS

I.

Rocking Mad Max Rockatansky on
the '73 Falcon XB might be all silence
with bleeps of radar sound crackling
through the radio static but this

motherfuc-shut-your-damn-mouth
told those pencil-pushing fools Fifi and
Labatouche that he was out of the game—
out, gone and full disillusioned

with the whole thing—and it would be
their limp-dicked fault for insisting
on a beachside holiday far away
for the missus and the Sprog, to clear the airs

in his hairs. Didn't they know Aussie-dystopian,
post-apocalyptic winds would
blow the bad stuff in its exfoliating sands
every which way and specially theirs?

That gang wasn't counting on that level
of anger! On Hammurabian precision.
Oh vivid Technicolor, Toecutter's fucking
eyes popped before he went splat!

II.

The '68 Mustang GT holds the same
contempt for rules like its driver.
The V8's purr is a direct injection
from McQueen's white-knuckle grip.

From home to hotel to morgue—
Lombard's switchbacks like discarded
paper floating in light wind—
the action caught by the Arriflex;

the burnt rubber real, noxious.
There's no glitter here, no morning-after call,
no I love you; this is nothing but guts.
Stomach-churning leaps, the screech

of brakes engaged ferocious like
Saint Mark's winged lion—the transferred
energy from the pavement an
immediate world, violent at 115 mph;

regardless of jazz, aware of flesh.
Jingoism entrenched at the helm;
can he flip his switch with ease?
Will he smile when the screen goes dark?

UMBRAL

Sweet Orinoco water breeze in his hair,
Tio Chicho would smile his marble-slab teeth
through the bushes of Zanjón Park.
He'd point with the wild pantomime
expected from those who are touched,
in the general direction of the
Orinocómetro when the tide was high,
when the tide was low.
Maybe he imagined the Carib demigod
Amalivaca sacrificing maidens
to the great anaconda Lalikilpará—
the *criollo* ouroboros.
Maybe the cars zipping past
on the Avenida Guzmán Blanco pissed him off.
Maybe he whispered to himself
the few lines of sanity he had left:

Oh life, three-fourths gone now;
my childhood in shadows
and my adolescence asphyxiated.
I'm on fire now, everything spacious
about me behind locked doors—
this threshold keeps turning into
a vacuum as it circles in on itself.

THE BOULDERS OF PARQUE ZANJÓN AT MIDNIGHT

Chicho's friends at night
are not the sloths he imagines
nor the gorgeous trees he's
dressed up with his brother's linens

or the sweet white flesh
of the *pumarosas* he found
unattended on the Araber's cart—
his friends are the many large

boulders that live in the park,
his burly protectors from an angry
earth borne; if mighty *tepuis*
house the gods, then these are

the rocks that prop open
the doors to their homes;
but they're his rocks and to him
they're always ready and impeccable

in what people now call that
old gangster-suit look from the '40s,
and while the folks staying
the night at the Amor Patrio

or Doña Carol *posadas* across
the way might find his night
peculiar or worth smacking down
with a hammer, Chicho and

his friends know it will rain soon
and the golden fire from that
rum bottle they found unattended
at the liquor store will keep

them warm, and that there's
enough of the stuff to go around
if the sloths and the trees
decide to drop by, oh yeah.

Let's take a minute here… let's look back at that first motorvator, that hep María Lionza and her sweet little tapir. Let's see how her story been told since days of yore.

MARÍA LIONZA RIDES HER LITTLE TAPIR INTO TOWN

I.

María Lionza's sculpted body greets us every Sunday night
when my dad tools the 30 into Caracas—the salty sand

strong on my hands, La Guaira's beaches a memory buried
by passing mountain and slick asphalt. Floral offerings always

surround her concrete pedestal, wads of rapidly depreciating
Bolívares jammed into nooks and crannies, dotting the

Francisco Fajardo like sad confetti. The devout followers
of her cult risk their lives crossing four lanes of speeding traffic

to beg her help. They offer orchids—always in bloom,
the chiseled stone of the statue cast in dramatic shadows

by the textured chiaroscuro of headlights and multicolored
votive candles—her arms raised, the skeletal pelvis in her hands,

the tapir's frozen strut brutalist in weight; strangely clean
of motor exhaust or industrial soot—a mother of pearl glow.

II.

They ran away, like spooked children
when the green-eyed girl jumped
out of the lake, her feet splashing

soft white spray and the unyielding
snap of a hundred piranhas.
All along they'd known those eyes

meant trouble and here was proof.
Tapirs and jaguarundi rushed to her,
foamy mouthed spider monkeys heralding

21

her might—orchid bloom in low brush
to half-moon jungle canopy booming
with news of a newborn divinity.

The Caquetio misunderstand, they
mustn't fear her, the Great Anaconda
did not reject the girl's sacrifice.

The very eyes that foretold doom
will bridge nature and humanity,
native and foreign; mortal, everlasting.

III.

The Jirjana people of Yaracuy knew for decades
that green eyes meant trouble.
Shamans labored over the meaning of this
and the Great Spirit revealed
that if a girl was born with this affliction,
they should prevent her from witnessing herself
in a reflective pool and, of course,
years before the Spanish barreled through—
such a girl was born.

Her father, heartbroken, kept the birth secret
and posted 22 guards outside her cave
to raise and protect her. His one directive,
aside from keeping their hands to themselves,
was that she never sees her own reflection.
The day the Spanish forces broke
through the natural barriers of Yaracuy and
decimated the Jirjana, all those guys,
of course, had fallen asleep
and the girl wandered off to a nearby lake.
Her soft eyes undulating in the liquid mirror
as her body grew into the astronomical
proportions of a giant snake,
rolling over every Spaniard between Acarigua
and Valencia—fulfilling the Great Spirit's prophecy.

IV.

When Yara was born—before the steel-tipped men
with coarse beards breached Yaracuy—her beautiful
green eyes brought hope to the tribe; their emerald
an amulet for her village, far too special to leave exposed.
So, she lived amongst the orchids and rivers of Sorte,
guarded by beauty, serenaded by the soft light of night.
The troubles began when the wind whispered news,
and passing beasts confirmed them, that the Spanish
situation was rapidly becoming a problem and would
require handling. She unburdened herself of the boar,
the tapir, the toucan—loyal sentries she wouldn't want
harmed and set out to meet the fair-skins; naïvely
believing that the civility of conversation would help
reach a diplomatic accord. To ease the proceedings and
knowing that strangers often mistrusted strangers,
she morphed to what they knew and introduced herself
as María del Prado to duplicitous Ponce de León—
everybody back home was counting on her, unaware
that the Spanish greed for gold was far greater than
her offer of peace and food could assuage; so she returned
to Sorte, her spirit broken, to reclaim her place amongst
the leaves and wonder if they'd been wrong about her eyes.

V.

Know that Mary didn't know how to swim—but loved the water.
Know that *onza* is Spanish for boar and that one was nearby.

With the boar gently nibbling on her chin, Mary remembers her
mother telling her to be careful, to watch her footing, distrust the beach.

The boar smells dusty, of earth but wet too, and it nudges her softly
to crawl higher up on the shore, closer to the dry driftwood.

Mary knows the boar is a friend—her friend—following wherever
she goes, alert to danger and continuously worried in her

absence; there's an understanding between them, the imperceptible
bond of love, not dominion. Weird and cute, joined at the hip.

VI.

María Alonso decided to stay in Barquisimeto
after she buried her husband because the farm
began to fall apart as soon as the gravediggers
smoothed the earth above him. Thinking it best

to drown her pain with work, she ignored
the customary five weeks of mourning and busied
herself turning the *hato* back to the profitable
operation it had once been—shocking her nosy

neighboring *rancheros* and their stuffy wives.
She raised wages and built homes for her workers
on fertile plots of land. She improved living
conditions for her animals too and soon had

over a thousand heads! Chivacoa, her favorite
boar, always trotted behind her horse when she
surveyed her lands, sniffing the air—orchids
blooming to the cry of *caricares* in her wake.

VII.

There were rats on that damn ship,
so María del Marqués didn't feel too

bad when the weather deteriorated
and split the vessel in half.

Her last memory, as the spume
consumed her, was how much

calmer the Caribbean was underneath.
There was no hurricane there.

Chivacoa, a young cacique,
was excited by the news his runners

brought, the water gods had
delivered a beautiful, fair-skinned

woman to his shores.
He would teach her the ways

of his people, the Jirjana, and make
her his queen. Together they

would rule over the impenetrable
mountains of Sorte and the beasts.

VIII.

The newspaper said the shamans were sure that your statue
in *la Autopista del Este* had split because Chávez was guilty

of crimes against nature and for strangling the country with
his lysergic communist rhetoric. That it was no mystery,

no atmospheric or seismic cause. That you'd been angered so
you suffocated Lake Maracaibo with un-killable duckweed.

These shamans, hardcore devotees of your cult—keepers
and worshippers of your Pantheon, your *potencias*—

los marialionceros, believe that you cut your veins in anger,
to bleed black blood. That you—queen, *criolla*, *Española*,

diosa india, wild, exotic, beautiful, *venezolana*—that you shine
your eyes from Sorte in these times of need.

Ay diosito, nos pasamos de raya y estamos a punto de ganarnos una coñaza. Mejor ponerse como el Payaso Popy y ver que pasa....

BETWEEN EL TIGRE AND THE DUMPING GROUNDS

Ahead of us a car's swaying in the sun,
the two lanes of road barely containing
the way it whips, a long dust cloud
held longer in the moisture of this heat—
chamos borrachos con el cheque de la semana,
the cabby says—and their car is nice,
nice for what passes for nice around these parts.
This is my grandfather's corner of the country,
though he never drove anything that nice,
and he was the town lawyer.
Lawyers and doctors though,
they don't drive anything that nice around here.
Tough work, *más que lo mio, la güebon'a—*
a mi me cuchillaron una vez, he adds.
Those boys gotta be divers,
vacuum-guiders for the diamond
and gold barges dredging the Caroní;
each floating village a citadel of foreign wealth,
a snail sliming sludge. Theirs is a slow death—
they drink their wages, marry *indias*
and breed all over the reservations
like the babies will avenge them.
I can picture the kids,
caricatured *mestizos* and *criollitos*;
loinclothed, mimic-playing aqualung hero.
Some of them try to hide diamonds
in their wetsuits when they're down in the muck,
held-breath capers of desperate braille—
they're usually the ones missing fingers.
Partial arms and nubby elbows
frosted by an ice-cold Polar.
Este pais se va a la mierda,
the cabby's not looking for a debate—
en el lodo, todos vamos a perder los dedos.

ALMA LLANERA
(after the traditional joropo by Rafael Bolívar Coronado)

We believe ourselves born from
the thunder of the river,
of vibrating emanations—
and that we're brethren to the foam,
the ibis, the rose, and the sun.
We call out wild names,
all female—and whoever answers
bulldozes through us
like wind between palm trees,
filling our primrose souls
with crystal clarity.
We love, we sing, and we cry,
as we dream of castanets
and the metronomic will by which
we set to tame our master's nag.

ARIA ON BOARD
(after Frank Giampietro's "Frankie the Haggler")

The Datsun's death was a spurt putt;
an unexpected tragedy on an off-ramp.

We couldn't have handled anything
beyond the reasonable expectation of

the motor's idle—you said the signs had
been there but I don't recall just how

conscious you were during that ride; the spilt
bag of candies certainly did not wake you

like keychain bumps when we sloped outta
Florida, but it's okay, we gonna get rested for

tomorrow cause wherever we arrive's gonna
burn and we won't be sad or stranded

any longer. Sometimes I feel like there'll be
more to suffer—like Hangin' Judge Parker is

scowling; fixin' to send big bad Bass Reeves,
unarmed, into injun' land after me.

CAN YOU AVOID SOMETHING YOU'VE NEVER SEEN?

I.
Since mother first mentioned
Chicho's story, in that odd
way she tells family tales,

like they're painful or embarrassing,
I've wondered what he thought
as the town's first automobile

ran him over as the sun hovered
over the plaza, its rays alive
on the Orinoco's roll.

I mean, I can't be sure
he even knew what a car was
since he's become a lackadaisical

myth—the crazy ass uncle who was
feared at every family party.
I don't know if he even heard

the crinkly dangle of the Model T's
front-mounted 177-cubic-inch,
inline 4-cylinder engine, I mean,

how fast could that damned thing
have gone? 35, 45 mph tops?

II.
I guess something
as foreign as that,
as alien even,
would have the
power to freeze
you in place, even
in 100-degree weather.

III.
Tia Carmen Teresa—with us in body but long gone in mind—
or Tia Aura, soul departed to wherever it was needed next;
would've been the ones to detangle all the whats-and-hows
of when it went down and—more importantly—bring linear
clarity to the quick decay of his sanity from promising young
stud to puzzling, but infinitely amusing, *criollo* village fool.
Now, the best we can hope for, is Carmen Teresa's daughter
(age and internet connections unknown) jogging her mind
if she ever gets to check her Facebook messages again.

IV.
If that Ford was the *guayanés* equivalent
of a locomotive careening out of control,
I'm shook and goosefleshed thinking
what would've been of him if say, my old man's
Renault 30, its 2.7 liter, PRV V6 engine
roaring like the Lyon-Paris *Train à Grande Vitesse*
on cocaine, had knocked him on his ass that day.

V.
Who could possibly have memories of family picnics now?
Any of Chicho's antics? What kinds of questions would form
on his brow if the Ford hadn't robbed him so? You boy! *¡Tú!*
*Ojos carmelita, hijo del árabe—¿sueñas ser abogado como
mi sobrino?* Wouldn't you rather have another cheese *arepa*, eh?
Leave some meat for the rest us? *¿Ya aprendistes a manejar?*

VI.
I bet if he hadn't gone crazy,
Chicho—that stud—would've ended up
with a nice girl like Sofía Silva, Miss Venezuela 1952,
the pride of *el estado* Bolívar.

VII.
There was a murmur among
        the patrons of the neighboring
                posadas: Amor Patrio, Doña Carol
                        and Don Carlos about the man

from Caracas who'd caused
       so much grief for the locals;
              that he was someone connected,
                  someone with friends;

and that he'd be gone that
       afternoon if he wasn't already.
              Some of the guests spoke slowly
                  over their *guayoyos*,

splitting their *arepitas* to soak
       in the steam, *disimulando que*
              no chismosiaban, but you know;
                  they were all talking shit.

VIII.
And they were talking it,
because the next morning

the rest of the town had
all the facts, spread with

wildfire speed by the three
lone chambermaids

employed in the triangle
of hospitality across from

Parque Zanjón and its
mighty boulders and

beautiful flowers. Oh yeah.
Everyone knew it was

the well-connected man
from Caracas with all of

his powerful city friends
who made the Model T

disappear, a cloud
of dust and horsehair

in its stead—no one knew
if the guy who got hit

survived, or worse,
lost his limbs, his eyes,

whatever—it didn't matter
because the man from

Caracas was gone gone gone
and every home within

spitting distance of the
Orinoco believed their own

version of what happened,
claro, after someone

first explained what a *carro* was.
Surely, they saw how funny it was

that the first one in town—on its
first casual cruise of the streets,

ran down the town's
finest-looking guy.

IX.
Letter from José Manuel Aliz (Chicho) to his beloved nephew César Obdulio
Iriarte (my grandpa) Ciudad Bolívar, Estado Bolívar, Venezuela – 1940's
(maybe)

Querido César,
Smile upon the motionless vegetables that surround your bed, the *abanico*
on your nightstand. Don't forget to look at the map on the wallpapered wall
before you leave for school each morning. Count the ceiling beams over and
over until you're confused—until you get lost and fall asleep between the
damp sheets of this fever. Remember that small canoe at the *hato*, the one
you dropped *pumarosas* into and forgot? How the fruit stained your
imagined maritime adventures? Take the time to breathe in the swell of the
patio under the palms, the warm breeze on that sea of tiles separating you
from the road; the smell of beasts and anthills from the forest. Whatever
you miss from home will resurface, whole, somewhere in your memories
when you need them most.

33

X.
More than anything,
what I would like to say is:
Chicho got trucked by a Ford,
and unrelated, mother
briefly drove a green Mustang 5.0
(crash and violence story some other time);
but my father—
he drove a Renault 30
after suffering the bad apple
built like a 1970 VW bug
and an LTD Classic, forever ruined
by too many turns coming back
from La Guaira upsetting
my *arepa*-filled stomach.

AT POSADA AMOR PATRIO, ACTUALLY

Lonely city,

narrow city, your faces dark;

how

do I face my own loneliness?

Can I steal away

from this angry town?

From dark faces?

Angered cries?

Will they rise

demanding apologies

from bloodied

bats?

THE PARK FOLLY OF YOUNG NONNA

Ciudad Bolívar, Estado Bolívar, Venezuela – 1942 (maybe)

Young Nonna, my mother's mother—blessed with a patience for schoolchildren and a knack for growing the best tomatoes and watermelons on the soil of her parent's borrowed land—arrives at Zanjón Park, her arms loaded with fresh clothes.

My mother—blessed more with a proclivity for the martial arts and debilitating allergies to kitchen work—doesn't factor here since she'd be the youngest of six (and the first one isn't even a plan for seeding in Nonna's belly yet).

Tio Chicho, my grandpa's (who is not my grandpa yet) uncle, saddened by the sloth's refusal, sits on a small hill overlooking the avenue. He has not been shaved since last Thursday—and only because Nonna brought a box of sweets and some cash from my grandpa (who is not my grandpa yet) to do so at Señor Vito's shop.

A woman and her son sit nearby. Kid's 6, maybe 7, hard to tell—the sun is high, and everything has a sparkle to it, but the woman definitely has a broken rosary in her purse. Far away, a war devours someone else's children.

And action!

What happened to the clothes I brought you last week? They told me at church that you were naked in the fountain. Again.

No no no niña, the sloth didn't like the shirts, so we tied them to the trees! Look over there! We made pretty dresses for the fancy party—all of these trees are invited but I'm a little cross the little bugger refused them—such nice cotton. We're hoping they have lots of candles around *la pista de baile*.

¡Pero Chicho, por Dios! You're going to get in trouble—again—if you try to dress them up...

I love their *borrachito* smiles.

Still, no excuse! And why were you in the fountain? You have to go home for your bath.

I take my bath whenever and wherever I want. Last week I showered with a Dubonnet Xenia! She was gorgeous!

No seas grosero, you have to stay away from cars.

36

Nonna looks off into the distance wondering if it's all worth it, this fuss over her boyfriend's crazy-ass uncle... how come no one else can do this shit? Chicho busies himself removing his pants—*¡Dios mío! Sín calzones*—as the child looks on...

¡Que desgracia! Y de una familia tan buena, says the mother as she manages to yoke the child into a half-twist behind herself as she pulls out the rosary from her purse...

(Note for light tech: move the 50' followspot from the mom to her movement with the beads, she'll be marked near a floor light so stop there)

Chicho, loving how sunlight hits the glass beads exploding from her purse and into all nooks and crannies of dry grass exclaims: *¡Señora! ¡Se le partió la cola a su rabipelao!*

(Nonna, exasperated) *Dolce Santa Regina, perchè mè, perchè?*

In her confusion, Chicho takes the clothes and flings them with a whirlwind motion:

Velutini says fire and water can mix without violence! That wind can build cities and I say you, you noble linens, I free you from the vileness of humanity's pores! Soak the sun! Soak the wind!

Perchè, perchè?

(Deus ex machina: scene freezes, stage goes dark, orchestral notes pending for Music Director)

        And action!

Nonna is dressed like the Corsican saint Julia of Nonza in airy robes—maybe light blue, maybe turquoise—she's holding a small palm frond and a wooden crucifix.

You poor, noble beast... you will rest soon. Your streets will be free of carburetor menaces.

She closes her eyes and thinks of how warm life will be once her cute *negrito* finishes his barrister studies in Trinidad.

Chicho, with a wink, turns to the audience and says:

Aha!

It would bring no justice to the parties
involved—all deceased now—to hold

a circus of this magnitude in a willing
court and since no one on this side of

things had the good sense of following
grandpa into the philosophies of law,

there's zero chance of guilting a high-nosed
cousin into pro bono work. Especially

against the might of legacy or the fancy
of holding a celebrity to an imagined

slight. Did Phelps, Sr. know his
consumer-driven invasion, to wit a

flotilla of Ford Model T's, be indirectly
responsible for injuries sustained a

decade later in a town over 600 kilometers
away? Would an incident of the sort,

namely the first car in town committing
the first hit-and-run during its maiden parade,

prevent Phelps, Sr. from establishing
himself in the country? How could we

bring Edgar Anzola into the fold?
After all, it was he (aged 16) who

learned all the ins-and-outs of the damned
car at the Ford Motor Co. assembly line in Detroit.

He was the connection, conning Phelps, Sr.
to invest in Venezuela with *criollo* grease monkey panache.

38

Should youthful impetus stand alongside
to these charges? And there's the

matter of legacy—how do we bend
history in our favor since Phelps, Jr.

(Venezuelan born) became first,
the leading authority on all things

avian in Venezuela, and to some degree,
the Americas; and second, the founding

father of Radio Caracas Televisión—
a defiant voice against the tyranny of

a rising narco-terrorist state? Should
everything be dismissed in hopes their

memories live exactly where they need
to live and be thankful all parties involved—

all whom loved this nation in their own
way and to their own ends—no longer

breathe to see how (for now) the commies
won and destroyed everything beyond

sanity, progress and peace?
Rilke wrote in his eighth letter to a young poet:

"...there is almost nothing I can say that will help you,
and I can hardly find one useful word."

PETRÓLEOS DE VENEZUELA, SOCIEDAD ANÓNIMA

What a giddy little git I must look
when I seek out the faces of other
customers at the pump as I imagine

them enjoying this nice, moist smell
of gasoline, regardless of octane,
going into the car. This simple,

dinosaur-based, flammable thing.
I feel good smelling it even as
electrical bombs go off in my brain

reminding me of all the negatives
this pumping action carries in the
greater scheme of things—good Lord,

and it's bad for your brain too,
to inhale it this deeply; letting it bite
crispy into the backs of my eyes;

how could I be the only one feeling
this swirl of petroleum euphoria?

WATCH OUT! MY MOTHER'S GOT A 5-POINT-O!

My old man, mostly because he loved my mother
but also loved his 30 so much he didn't want anyone else

messing with it, bought the then 20-something beauty
a dark green Mustang 5.0 to tear Caracas up.

Skip ahead to a month later—mom's picked me up
from school and as we idle in the center lane at a red light,

a white jitney goes wide for a right turn and scrapes
my door, tearing the rearview off with a cold metallic

screech—mom, who's never been much for being
taken for a ride—uttered the early '80s version of oh fuck no

and gunned after the jitney who, either unaware or misogynistic
in decision, kept his cruise uninterrupted, down *Calle Mucuchíes*.

       [My old man would prove, time and time again,
       that his style of driving was built for endurance,
       but this would be the only time mother popped
       the hood on her level of automobile crazy—if Craigslist,
       the dark web, or solid criminal contacts existed at the time,
       she would've been one Hell of a getaway driver]

It's a miracle and testament to her skills that nothing else
got wrecked that day; were we even wearing seatbelts?

Probably not; I remember sliding under the dash
after she caught up, nosed ahead and broke short

in front of it; how the jitney avoided accordioning us I'll never
understand. As I steadied myself on the shifter,

now flimsy in neutral, mom had jumped out with
Valkyrie fury jolting the taste of revenge coursing

through her Corsican blood—shit was incredible—
she kicked in the jitney's folding door and lunged

at the driver with a video game mix of palm strikes,
chops and, assisted by the overhead handrails,

a devastating front kick to the groin that caused the man
to half-double-up on himself and hit the steering wheel

with his face. The scene froze me—is this why my aunts
and uncles feared her? The youngest and most violent

of six? Was this why nonna lived in another city?
There was so much I didn't understand that day

and forgotten, that it wouldn't be until decades later,
at a family party in Miami, when my old man told the story,

mother at his side—stone face scowling—adding how weeks later,
the jitney's owner, the then five-star pride of Caracas,

the Hotel Tamanaco, called to say they had a check
for him to pick up. At the hotel lobby, for whatever

cruel reason, the driver—face bruised, spirit broken—was forced
to hand my dad the check, timidly asking,

    ¿Su señora no está aquí, no?

Renault30
Renault30*Renault30*
Renault30*Renault30*Renault30
Renault30Renault30Renault30*Renault30*Renault30
Renault30Renault30 Renault30 Renault30*Renault30*Renault30
Renault30Renault30Renault30Renault30Renault30*Renault30*Renault30
Renault30Renault30 Renault30Renault30Renault30Renault30*Renault30*Renault30
Renault30*Renault30*Renault30Renault30Renault30Renault30Renault30*Renault30*Renault30
*Renault30Renault30*Renault30Renault30Renault30Renault30**Renault30Renault30**
*Renault30Renault30*Renault30Renault30Renault30**Renault30Renault30**
*Renault30Renault30*Renault30Renault30**Renault30Renault30**
*Renault30Renault30*Renault30**Renault30Renault30**
*Renault30***Renault30**Renault30**
*Renault30***Renault30**
Renault30

DAD BATS CLEANUP IN TODAY'S LINEUP

This poem about my dad, shouldn't be better than
my dad or than being with my dad.
This poem shouldn't be better than the memory
of my dad hitting that homerun—with the bases
loaded—he predicted on the drive that
morning when he was getting irked by
his cousin (by marriage) Pedro's incessant questioning.
Primo, are you any good? ¿No estás muy gordito pa' jugar?
¿Primo, tu no trabajas en el banco, quién te invitó?
This poem shouldn't be better than Pedro's
confused amazement after the dinger
cleared the diamond and he triumphantly
waved a bird at him when he stepped on home plate,
the firm thud of his metal cleats for emphasis.
This poem is about my youth, my father's adulthood
and Pedro being quiet on the ride home.
But it's also about the car, the Renault 30, my favorite, a fine
sand-colored hatchback sedan that got us there and back.

CODA (NOT-SO-SAVAGE DETECTIVE)

I.

The search for loncar began after I wrote a thank you note but couldn't find where to send it. So we flew to Michigan after saving some cash and decided to let the kindness of strangers and nature lead the way. First, we took a bus out to Julia Moore's childhood homestead, a remarkably beautiful farm long relieved of daily duty. Other than scenery and rusted equipment we mistook for outsider art, there wasn't much. Decided on Kalamazoo next, since we had seen a kid earlier fiddling with a plastic kazoo outside of a knickknack shop and thought it was a sign—but mostly cuz it sounded like an amusing place. Can't say much came from that, really, but we spotted someone who fit the description of NEA fellow Larissa Szporluk at a coffee shop on Burdick Street. After that we figured we'd have to tick Roethke off the list as a possible source before we could continue but were a little flabbergasted by the Michigan youth who'd let his memory wither; gotta say, that fueled some heavy drinking before we made it to Detroit hoping a little visceral Daniels would do us some good and help refocus the search. Learned from a former assembly line worker, who was remarkably happy to talk shop 'bout the old days, that Daniels had skipped the Motor City years back— something we forgot to google in our drunken haze to be honest. After that embarrassing setback we learned we could review some of Vernon Cole's papers held in a private collection in Flint. The ornery quack doctor's letters to former lovers and eternal detractors didn't reveal much other than his taste for wine began well before he jumped the pond.

II.

1983 – Richard Tillinghast (no relation to the risk managers), is hired for poetics of the nascent MFA program at the University of Michigan. Program is known for developing strong voices and for avoiding marketable trends like Midwestern surrealism, "language" poetry, the New Formalism, the New Narrative, etc. Known contact with loncar (aka Michael Loncar then) at "contentious and memorable workshop" (so say RT and fellow attendees) in the early '90s.

2018 – Individual's (same name) obit is found through a cursory online search. Assumed to be a different person due to age at time of death but Iowa location raises suspicions of poetics. Well-liked and survived by a large family, he is fondly remembered for a delicious bean dish that was the Cadillac comestible of his neighborhood block parties.

45

1997 & 1999 – IMDB lists two short films, possibly visual poetic exercises, credited to a de-stylized "M. Loncar." Mostly B&W work and the titles match (or at least evoke a feeling of undebatable similarity) poems from sole published manuscript. YouTube user, nansen's cat, uploads both videos—previously unshared—hidden within a playlist of '90s Ann Arbor shoegazers Naming Mary, sometime in the fall of 2019.

1999 – Personal copy of *66 galaxie* purchased in May for $11.95 (stamped) at original Books & Books, Coral Gables location.

2015 – Richard "Richie Rich" Lopez recalls accidental discovery at his public library through poetry anthology in a since untended blog. Gives glowing review of manuscript (note: winner of Katharine Bakeless Nason Poetry Prize), questions—as we all have—what has happened and suggests electronic publishing and print-on-demand as perfect avenues for loncar's poesy to flourish. In 2018, a comment by Blogger user "m" replies:

Thanks for this Richard!! I appreciate it! m)

No further exchanges recorded in the ether.

III.
We didn't think Lansing would be much of an inroad, but wouldn't you know it! Laura Ulewicz, the hippie from automotive unions-borne, left a chemtrail through town we were able to pick up after a night of blotter. In a quiet room near the Foster Library, we drew shapes in the sand and listened—really listened—and learned we'd be protected by lucidity from desolation if it became too late to undertake the rest of this journey. We had to liberate this knowledge as servants of invented devices, infected by a desire for power. Her papers exalted the hippie idealism that drove her West, but the nostalgia mathematically placed within her words reminded us that poetry belongs to the crowd, to the relative, to the virtual, to the illusory. We hopped on a bus to Ann Arbor the next morning, a Saturday, lysergically drowned in multiplicity, looking for burning stones, walking trees, and the songs of wind towers. Knowing we'd have to let the unseen lead us, we found the center of UMich the following morning and meditated until Jane Kenyon, the muse, entered our souls: *the blossom pressed in a book, found again after two hundred years...* and I guess the lesson here, in order to suppress the urge to dominate without merit, is if you write something but can't figure out where to send it, it's probably better to put it in a drawer—preferably under something heavy—and let someone else come down the

line and make better sense of it all. One thing's for sure, friend, I'm not going back to Venezuela anytime soon and if and when I do, whole place is gonna look like I was teleported to a different planet. I know now I'll never find an exact replica of my father's 30 and I'm happy with the version that lives in my heart. We're off now, ready to put this chapter behind us and hop on the next Mini Moke, Fiat Uno, or electric Twizy (if we can find one decently priced in this orange wasteland) life throws our way and run afoul of pimps, cops, whatever....

It's never too late to purchase the eBook version of this... if you do, you could be clicking below and getting your very own copy of the fell codex that inspired this mess. Have fun typing this bullshit out:

https://www.amazon.com/66-Galaxie-Poems-Bakeless-Prize/
dp/0874518776/ref=sr_1_1?keywords=m+loncar&qid=1637180852&qsid=1
34-4078168-4468169&rnid=2941120011&s=books&sr=1-1&sres=08745187
84%2C1887672044%2C9619403193%2C9619345223%2C9619403177

MAGNETIC DOGGEREL #1

The new bright mother blossoms minutely,
bright white as if flaked with fake snow.
The century ends, stars are less, and yet
everything willfully rises eternal and ice dry,
rising after the equinox day you'll ask why
the seasons ebb and where ice floes flow.
Seeing it through, you've armed yourself
with moon tides slicing clean and falling dark.
Earth bounty, warm night—when did those
freckles on your cheek triangulate into the
summer solstice of Deneb, Vega, and Altair?
Sky! Sun! My! You're gonna have to bring
your thigh closer than 16,000 light years.
I will shower short, like summer, and
unlike nature, you will not leave. No. You'll
let clouds rain using the slow turn until
gray and wrinkled, you pat the dirt on me.

IN FRANCE WITH THE FRENCH

The first time I tried tomato juice was when I was 13 and over-bougie'd at the Pan Am Clipper Club at JFK ahead of a transatlantic jump to the Côte d'Azur. That cold V8 can poured over ice with a twist of lime was deee-vine and ever the excessive, I must've had five or six of the suckers, each tart lycopene bomb more delicious than the last. Needless to say, in a funky future echo of my eventual graduation to Bloody Mary's, my stomach was a bombed-out Beirut by the time we flew past the Corner Islands.

Now, that was a long time ago and I'm having a hard time remembering if my old man decided to rock his youthful energies behind the wheel of the rental the morning we landed in Nice or that afternoon—only thing I'm sure of is I had to get to the hotel first, and he looked pretty jet-lagged.

It was outside of the Pullman Hotel's entrance, and at the behest of the animated Italian working the door – *Avanti la macchina, avanti la macchina!* – that I became aware of the Lancia Thema's shortcomings. It wasn't my old man not realizing the bellman was hollering at him but the damn car failing to cooperate forth from my dad's soft shoe routine on the clutch and accelerator to the veiny petrol and electric circuits of its Torino-forged body. Yeah, the damn *macchina* chose not to move.

But we took the charcoal grey rental out to the surrounding villages and towns of Nice for a drive, my old man gunning the Italian economy sedan like it was one of its higher-end automotive *cugini* through narrow cliff roads; my mom periodically asking him to slow down, that all three kids were in the car—but it didn't matter, he knew what he was doing, jet-lagged or not.

It was a beautiful drive, whatever demon turmoil bubbled-up my guts earlier washed away by the crisp breeze from the Baie des Anges.

In his youth, my old man was a master of vacationing and these first hours on the Côte were already pointing to short nights and long, packed days of non-touristy touristing. We were all feeling that excitement in the car as we cruised down La Promenade des Anglais back to our hotel, when he whispered an uh-oh... an uncharacteristic blip of nerves for a guy who es- caped communism twice and worked in Caracas' worst slum clinics sewing and patching up thugs who could very well return the favor with a box of car parts or a pistol-whip mugging in the parking lot.

The sun was on its slow set. Something was wrong. Something had given out. And we were coming up on a red light.

He did everything he could to stop the car – downshifting and engaging the handbrake little by little – finally maneuvering the beast over the small concrete siding of La Prom, narrowly avoiding the pedestrian light post before crashing to a halt into one of the white concrete rails in the dying shadow of the Le Negresco Hotel's magnificent pink cupola.

That's when he realized that in the excitement of his first (and to date, only) automobile accident, he didn't miss the coupe that was waiting at the light, grazing its bumper and cracking its rear passenger taillight. The slightest of nicks compared to the smoking crater that had appeared where most of the Lancia's front had been.

After checking we were okay, he muttered a soft *a la verga*, the *criollo* version of an oh fuck as a pair of gallic biddies exited the coupe, craning their bodies every which way and rubbing their necks. Didn't think we'd see this kind of American display in France – and specially not from the French – but here we were.

This didn't look good, but my old man was confident he could sort things out since he spoke French. I'll keep this part short since I want to get to the punchline and a pair of heroes appear to potentially steal my old man's thunder (but in a good way).

The first was an old man walking his dog who told my dad he saw everything—meaning the herculean efforts to avoid a catastrophe—and had used a payphone to call the cops. The second was the young gendarme who took the call, crisp in his uniform and sure of his policing future, who told the biddies he wasn't calling "a fucking ambulance" and to "get back in the car" while he wrote this up. Thank heavens we were in France with some of the French who hadn't been poisoned by American litigious lust.

Everything did get sorted out, eventually. The Lancia's breaks were shit. The biddies went on their merry way, unharmed, knowing the rental company would fix their minor damages. The man with the *chien* bid us adieu, asking—nay, imploring—us to enjoy the rest of our stay in his marvelous country, and the cop said we should walk back to the hotel since La Prom was better enjoyed on foot.

The night sky on the Côte d'Azur was beautiful; summer stars visible as soft waves eroded our jacked-up nerves. Whatever animosity might've risen against the biddies melted as we walked back.

I couldn't help but think how things would've turned that day if we had rented a different car. The stars, blinking like the hundred eyes of Argus Panoptes, reminded me of the Victor Vasarely designed diamond logo that adorned dozens of grills on the rental lot that morning.

Dammit dad, thank you for everything, but you should've rented a Renault.

POSTSCRIPT: CONFESIÓN

It's a kind of truth that William Henry Phelps
had the greedy "Ford rhymes with lord"
line on his lips that day as deckhands
secured his boat, but it is the poetic truth—
and one paid into silence
by the marketing department
of a company I will soon mention—
that a young Yago S. Cura,
scolded scion of James Tate's terrible anger,
scribbled the very same line in a
moleskin notepad (under the haze
of whatever shake he'd bought
from the ambulatory dorm-room-goods
salesman he knew) on a short list of quick wits
for the Ford Motor Co. to consider,
as a slow breeze shuffled through
the buildings of the UMass Amherst campus.

Notes

TO BE FAIR
El día de parada – "stoppage day" was implemented on May 14, 1979, in Caracas as a traffic and contamination mitigation strategy. Depending on the last number of a car's license plate, it couldn't be operated on certain days. Of course *criollísmo* ideology fought this notion with large sums of cash exchanging hands across slivers of plexiglass across the city. To some unnamed, low-level bureaucrat's credit, Venezuela was the first nation in Latin America to try out this progressive strategy.

HUGO CHÁVEZ JOINS TWITTER ON APRIL 2010
Sadly, most of these are true from an account that, against all odds – and supported by idiotic ideology – continues to exist.

ALMA LLANERA
A song best enjoyed wearing a *liqui liqui* under a palm tree, surrounded by littoral breezes.

ARIA ON BOARD
Frank's a solid guy. One of the few who understands that if you're gonna read poems at a bar in Miami, you might have to deal with idiot drunks.

ESTATE OF J.M. ALIZ V. WILLIAM PHELPS ORNITHOLOGICAL COLLECTION
William Henry Phelps, Jr. (Dec. 25, 1902 – Aug. 13, 1988) was a Venezuelan ornithologist, businessman, and national treasure. He published over 70 books on the birds of Venezuela, and in 1953, founded Radio Caracas Televisión, one of the most important TV stations in Venezuela – destroyed by the imbecile Chávez in 2007.

Adapted from Rainer Maria Rilke's *Letters to a Young Poet (Letter 8)*, Aug. 12, 1904

DAD BATS CLEANUP IN TODAY'S LINEUP
Of all the times I went with my dad to see him play softball, of all the homeruns he belted over the fence, this one sticks out for its *Babe Ruth-esque* qualities.

CODA (NOT-SO-SAVAGE DETECTIVE)
Adapted from Jane Kenyon's "Briefly It Enters, and Briefly Speaks"

POSTSCRIPT: CONFESIÓN

Not sure how terrible his anger might've been but let's be clear about one thing, no Pulitzer Prize can hide the "Anthony Hopkins as Hannibal Lecter" look of a very young, and very eager James Tate.

www.ingramcontent.com/pod-product-compliance
Lightning Source LLC
Chambersburg PA
CBHW070937120626
46546CB00004B/1452